The
Womanual

A non-owner's guide to repairing and maintaining a working relationship.

by Dan Mielke

The Womanual

Womanual

A non-owner's guide to repairing and maintaining a working relationship.

by Dan Mielke

Published By

ATHANATOS
PUBLISHING GROUP

The Womanual:

A non-owner's guide to repairing and maintaining a working relationship.

by Dan Mielke

ISBN 978-1-936830-82-4

Published by Athanatos Publishing Group

www.athanatosministries.org

Author website:

www.womanual.us

Also available as an audio book. See website for details.

Foreword
Introduction

Foreword:

As a woman, let me be the first to say how confusing and unfair women can be. I apologize to all of you men on behalf of the fairer and more complicated sex. All too often we women make it almost impossible for a man to read us, let alone lead us. We often say one thing while meaning another. We cry for reasons indiscernible to you and to us. We talk forever about nothing when we're happy, or refuse to say a word when we're angry. We spend your money, and then complain you don't care about our needs.

We are a complex gender. This is why I value my husband's willingness to take up the charge to follow I Peter 3:7, *"Likewise, ye husbands, dwell with them (your wives) according to knowledge, giving honor unto the wife, as unto the weaker vessel."* This a difficult task.

Many would like to say that the sodomite movement has crippled marriage today. Yet, sexual perversion is just a symptom. Marriages built without understanding have actually paved the way for these perversions to become accepted. Men have found it easier to communicate with men, and women have grown tired of waiting for men to understand.

The church stands up to fight against immorality, while giving a terrible picture of what true marriage ought to be. Husbands and wives have failed to follow God's command of understanding one another. Christian marriages are failing, and it is no wonder the world doesn't want to follow our model.

While out with some girlfriends, the topic of our husbands came up. My friends complained, razzed, and emasculated their husbands with every word. Anger, manipulation, and sarcasm dripped from their tongues. One of them turned to me and asked, *"What about you Christa, what's your husband like?"* I didn't want to make all these women feel bad, but honestly, I didn't have anything to complain about.

My husband takes his responsibility to lead our home very seriously. I didn't know what to say. Finally, I said, "My husband is the most convicting person to live with. He's always pointing me to Jesus, and I'm so grateful for his humble leadership. He's the most Christ-like person I've ever met." Surprise and longing filled the eyes of the women staring back at me. It was in that moment I knew my husband needed to share his secrets of leading our home.

As the recipient of the practical application of the truths in this book, I can say with satisfaction and confidence that inside these pages lies the key to understanding the mysteries of womanhood in such a way as to glorify God. If applied, the truths found in the Womanual will transform your marriage.

Christa Mielke

Happy wife and mother

Introduction

To my fellow guys,

The fact that you are reading a manual shows you are serious about serving your wife. Your actions show that you are interested in making your marriage a success. Whether you are reading this to fine tune an already wonderful relationship, or trying to understand, "What went wrong?" I pray that your wife will see the effort you are taking at this moment to better your marriage.

In plain-man terms we are going to look at the seemingly impossible inner workings of a woman. Women are complex, yet if men take the time, they are understandable. May the truths in this book help you better serve your wife, as you learn to understand her.

Chapter 1
A Word from the Manufacturer
The man's role and responsibility: to lead and understand

We are going to be examining the complicated machine of woman, and delineate our responsibility as men. **If you are a woman and planning on reading this book, you must realize this book is written to help you, but not intended for you to read.** You will be compared to things guys find beautiful and can understand, like trucks and engines.

The problems that arise in marriage are not the responsibility of the female. You may be surprised to hear this, but this will come as no surprise to the women who, despite my previous warning, are still reading this book. Before we delve into the responsibilities of the husband, we must first take a look at the foundations of marriage.

> **It must be remembered that God made you the mechanic, and He gave you all the information you need.**

God created marriage in order to show a picture of the unity of God (Gen 1:26, Eph 5:25). Mankind was made to live in perfect harmony with God and each other. Unfortunately, mankind thought they knew better than an all-powerful God and blatantly disobeyed God. For a more detailed account, see Genesis 3:1-16. Because of their rebellion, not only was their relationship with God destroyed, their relationship with each other was also affected (Gen 3:16). Since that day, mankind has fought God and each other because of sin. This factory defect, imprinted into the first married couple, has been multiplied ever since and exists in every individual and every marriage.

This defect has corrupted all of creation, and rocked the world with its horrendous consequences (Rom 8:22). The worst part of sin is that it destroys mankind's reason for existence. Mankind was created to have a relationship and image God, yet sin bars humanity from a relationship with a holy, perfect God. Without the ability to have a relationship with the Creator, God would have had to recall all of creation and send it to recycling. Thankfully, God had prepared a plan of deliverance and a way of peace even before He made the world (I Pet 1:20).

> **Your marriage will never be closer than your relationship with Jesus Christ.**

Through the death of Jesus, God was able to fix the broken relationship with His creation, because in Jesus' death, the penalty for sin had been paid (Rom 6:23). God asks for each individual to repent of rebellious sin and come to Him in faith. Acts 16:31: "And they said, 'Believe on the Lord Jesus Christ, and thou shalt be saved, and thy house.'"

This belief is shown through trusting completely in Someone greater than ourselves: Jesus Christ. It is the acknowledgment that I am hopelessly broken and in need of repair because of my sin. This submission to God not only brings peace between God and us, but it also gives the model of peace to be emulated between our wives and us.

My marriage will never be closer than my own relationship with God. If I cannot flawlessly follow a God who is perfect, why would I expect my wife to follow me when I am far from perfect?

It is a sobering thought to realize that everything done to your wife is done to the bride of Christ.

After restoring the broken relationship with God (salvation), mankind is not only able to have a relationship with a holy God, but we are able to have true meaning and purpose in everything we do. Eternal meaning in marriage is now possible.

This eternal meaning stems from the realization that marriage was designed to be a picture of the unity of God (Gen 1:26-28). The equal worth and distinct roles of husband and wife reflect back a mirrored image of the roles of the Godhead. Your marriage is a picture of an eternal relationship. Therefore, when a marriage is unified, God can be glorified.

This is key to a successful marriage. As both husband and wife are able to obediently follow God, by fulfilling their distinct roles, God is glorified. The end result is not simply a harmonious marriage, but a marriage that reflects the relation of Christ and His bride. Through a God-honoring marriage people are able to see what God looks like.

God has made it explicitly clear that men are to be the servant leaders of their homes (Eph 5:18-33). "For the husband is the head of the wife, even as Christ is the head of the church: and he is the savior of the body." (Eph 5:23) In guy terms, that means that anything that goes wrong is our job to prevent or fix. It must be remembered that God made you the mechanic, and God gave you all the information you need for a wonderful and fulfilling marriage.

If you are married or pursuing marriage, God has entrusted you with a great privilege and responsibility. Just as Christ is working on the church (Eph 5:25-27), God has put you in a position as a husband to take care of His property. He has given you the keys, He wants you to pop the hood, inspect the engine, and have her in better running order than when He dropped it off.

If you are going to have a smooth operating machine, it takes dedication and the commitment that you will continue. You cannot get into the inner workings of a woman and then decide to quit. You must not leave your wife stranded like the muscle car you started to fix up and then left unfinished on blocks until it rusted away. If you want to fulfill the duty for which God called you and imitate Christ, you the mechanic are going to have to commit yourself.

You may be thinking, "I already am committed to my wife. I work insane hours, provide a roof over her head, protect her, stay faithful to her; if that's not commitment, what is?" Commitment goes far deeper than simply providing the physical needs of our spouse; it involves meeting the emotional and spiritual needs as well. Imagine if God provided only for our physical needs. What would that mean for our eternal souls?

Our commitment to God and our wives is shown by our commitment to understand our wives. God commands husbands in I Peter 3:7, "Likewise, ye husbands, dwell with them according to knowledge, giving honor unto the wife, as unto the weaker vessel, and as being heirs together of the grace of life; that your prayers be not hindered." The admonition to understand our wives is a direct command for all husbands, and one to which very few are willing to commit. Just as the God-ordained difference of a woman's body is fulfilling to her husband, the journey of understanding the emotional and spiritual differences of our wives is equally fulfilling.

God commands real men to honor their wives by understanding them.

In I Peter 3:7, God does not give an exemption clause. Not only are men commanded to understand their wives, a curse is attached to men who are not seeking to understand. If husbands are not willing to follow God in faith and believe the truths that He has laid forth in His Word, it should be no surprise that the blessings of God have stopped. If a husband is not actively seeking to commit to knowing and understanding his wife, according to I Peter 3:7 he is not committed to following God.

Let me challenge you. If you are to live out your commitment to God and seek to lift the curse attached to your marriage or prevent the curse from entering your home, you must commit to understanding your wife. I pray this Womanual will assist you in your pursuit of a fulfilling and God-centered marriage.

Man Challenge:

I _____ hereby commit to honoring my God by being the husband He called me to be, and vow to love, serve and understand my wife. Date _____

Chapter 2
Know Your Machine
The uniqueness of her operating system

Women are beautiful. If they weren't, there would not be over seven billion people inhabiting this planet. Women are beautiful because God made them that way. Do you realize that God custom-designed the woman you live with just for you? In Genesis 2:15 man was put in the garden to work, and in verse 20 Adam does work, but God knew we needed a little more than just a goal, so He custom-made the crowning star of His creation, woman. The warmth of the sun, the power of a river, the gentle rain - all are shared by so many animals. Even a sunset is seen by all of God's living creatures, but a woman is designed especially for one man.

If you were to go to a car dealer, you have to pay top dollar for a custom vehicle, and every single feature would cost you. Yet God has given you a priceless treasure that He planned for you in your wife. She completes you. The man that God pronounced as good, Adam, still needed something. Often times we men complain that we wish our wives would understand or think like a guy, but that is not what we really want, because sameness would mean we lose the specialness which God created in a woman. That would be like wishing a painting were all one color; that would not complete the picture. In fact, sameness would detract. We as men need to recognize that in the difference lies the beauty.

Women are different for a reason; therefore, I must be willing to understand that "differentness" in order to fulfill my commission from God. God made men as protectors, women as nourishers; God made men as conquerors, women as peacemakers, etc. Because of the God-ordained difference in roles, women operate on a different system. Men are commanded to understand this system.

> You cannot blame the vehicle for stalling if it is low on fuel.

The woman's operating system must be understood in order for peak performance. In my teen years I began working at a salvage yard. I had not grown up around heavy equipment, and the junkyard was full of them. It did not take long for me to make a fool of myself on multiple occasions. One such occasion after I had learned to operate the Bob Cat skid steer, I noticed the fuel was low. So I told the co-worker that we would need some more gas. He laughed at me and said, "It takes fuel, not gas." I thought he was being a little too ornery that day, but he was right. It took fuel, and nobody would have been happy if I had put gas where diesel fuel belonged.

The woman's operating system compliments, yet is not interchangeable with, the man's. Most guys run on action, adventure, and success; women are fueled more by their emotions. We might rant and rave about how silly this fact is in women, but it will not change the fact that a diesel engine is designed to burn diesel fuel. You would not complain that when you fuel a semi you have to go to a different fueling pump; you accept the fact that a semi is different than a geo metro and act accordingly.

The first thing that must be understood by men is that women work on different fuel, and the husbands are required to keep the tank full. If you haven't bothered to refuel your machine, it will not work. You cannot blame the vehicle for stalling if it is low on fuel.

Females are fueled by emotion. A husband is there to fill up her emotional tank, and since you are her "station" to fill up, you had better be prepared for the amazing effects of a woman who has her emotional needs met. Every area of a woman's life is affected by her emotions. Once I realize what fuel my wife runs on, and I keep her tank full, frankly there have been nights where I had to be the one telling her I had a headache.

Your differences are God ordained, and so is your understanding.

Emotions are a huge need in a wife's life. If I cannot respect the needs of my wife, she has no standard by which to respect me. Fulfilling the obvious requirements of a husband (shelter, food, staying sexually faithful), without meeting the emotional needs of your wife, is no different than keeping an immaculate interior in your vehicle without putting fuel into the tank.

Men fail miserably in the fulfilling of a woman's emotions. This problem often is not due to lack of effort on the man's part. What man has not felt the intense desire to please his wife blow up in his face after yet another failed attempt to understand and please his wife? Like salt from the road, failure after failure soon whittles away at the man's resolve, and he concludes that it is useless to try and saves his energy and his heartache for other projects. The strain of continued failure is too much. If you are in this boat, take heart: This book will help you crawl out. If you have not gotten to the horrid land of apathy, the principles in this book, if applied, will keep you from ever getting close.

Chapter 3
Filling the Tank

EMOTIONS

E   F

Meeting your wife's emotional needs through protecting, pampering, praising

On Sunday, God's day of rest, you will often find people scrambling out the door, moms dutifully changing soiled outfits that moments earlier were clean and spotless, children's clothes scattered across the floor, half eaten corn flakes soaking in a bowl of warm milk, and the occasional call to promptness coming from the impatient driver, all combining to make the arrival at Sunday school quite an ordeal.

Such was the scene one Sunday morning as my wife and I hurried out to our white Chevy minivan. We pulled into the alley mentally debating whether it would be right to speed in order to get to church in time, when the engine suddenly sputtered, and all was silent. I restarted the engine only to hear a tremendous screech. I called my brother, who lived 5 miles away, and in ten minutes we were on our way to church, arriving only fashionably late. At church, I received quite a lot of information from self-proclaimed mechanics regarding our stranded van. These fixes ranged from loose battery terminals to total-engine overhauls.

That night a friend of mine came to see if he could diagnose the problem. His headlights illuminated the makeshift sign that hung from our window: "Engine Died." After forty-five minutes of tests and pinched fingers, we concluded it was the fuel pump. The part would cost several hundred dollars and labor would be comparable. As we were clearing a place on the lawn to store the vehicle until morning, my friend crawled under the van and started pounding, and the van started right up. The van soon died, so I ran to the garage, grabbed a gas can and put a small amount of gas in the tank. When I turned the key, it turned over and purred like a kitten (a really big 6,500 lb. kitten). It turned out that what we thought would be a major expense and costly repair was only a faulty gas gauge, and we were unknowingly running on empty.

This scenario is played over and over in most marriages. The husband is frustrated that his wife isn't working (disrespectful, nagging, not supportive, lack of sex, etc.). Eventually the husband comes to the conclusion that if she would just change... life would go smoothly, and the problem is the wife's fault.

If we as husbands were to take a step back and look at the situation, most of the problems in our marriage are because we didn't put enough fuel into the tank. The ways life drains our wives are endless but if the tank is full, it is a fun ride.

No self-respecting man would send his wife on a road trip with an empty tank. Yet it is standard for Christian husbands to daily expect their wives to operate on an empty emotional tank, and they do little to fill it. It is a husband's duty to keep the tank full (I Peter 3:7). Because of the different fuel required in a woman, a woman's tank is not filled the same way as a man's.

EMOTIONS

Women's emotional needs are met in three distinct areas. They need praise, protection, and pampering. We will look closely at each aspect of our responsibility.

Women need praise. Women are constantly made to feel insecure and are screaming to feel the praise and adoration of their husbands. Husbands are to follow the pattern set forth by God of confirming the position of believers (Rom 8:1, Eph 1). They need praise for all aspects of who they are. A good husband will follow Proverbs 31:28 in regard to praise. "Her children arise up, and call her blessed; her husband also, and he praiseth her." Your wife craves praise for her body. Tell her specifically what you adore about her body, what it makes you feel when you see her, how you can't get enough of her, stare at her, kiss her with no other intention, write her a note on the mirror.

She also needs praise for her spirit. The honor and respect you feel when your wife tells you how she admires your courage or hard work, is the same feeling your wife gets when you recognize the beauty of her soul. You married more than just a body; it came attached to a person. Praise her in public and in private for the beauty of who she is. When it comes to praise, remember it takes ten kind words to eradicate one harsh word.

Wives also need praise in the area of what they do. Take a moment to ponder all the tasks your wife does on a weekly basis. You may be surprised at the diversity of tasks your wife is involved in.

If you are more of a hands-on learner, spend your next day off doing all the responsibilities or chores you wrote down. You may be surprised how labor-intensive these tasks are, especially if you have children who systematically undo most chores.

After viewing the enormous amount of time my wife gives to me in just one area, I should be immensely grateful for what she does, and let her know specifically how I appreciate her act of love and support.

The second way a man can fill the emotional needs of his wife is through protection. Men are built to protect. Suppose you turned on the radio on your way to work and the broadcast was interrupted by an announcement that a known sexual offender had just escaped from an asylum and was seen near your house. What would you do? Whether or not what you do is legal, I would guarantee you would protect your family.

Women need praise, protection, and pampering.

Most men are good at physically protecting their wives. They protect them physically by providing a roof over their heads and financially by supporting them in many ways, but when it comes to protecting them inside the home, the wife is ravaged by her husband. Not only does a wife need protection from the outside, women need protection from the inside. A good husband must be willing to protect his wife from both inside and outside dangers.

Your wife needs to have her emotions protected by the one she loves. Women need to feel their emotions are vindicated. This emotional vindication on the surface may seem sil-

14

ly, but if we are honest, isn't that what men are asking for every time we want sex? Husbands need to realize that if they consistently belittle their wife's ideas or concerns (through sarcasm, mocking, talking down), the wife will begin to close up.

Emotions are what makes life exciting, if you do not protect them excitement will perish.

That means everything starts closing up: intimacy, laughter, concerns, everything. Why would a woman want to open up, knowing she will be criticized, ridiculed, or made fun of?

In order to protect the frail beauty of her emotions, a husband must learn not to say anything without first passing it through the filter, "Would God say this to my wife?"

Finally, in order to keep the tank full, a woman needs pampering (Ephesians 3:20). Pampering will only work if the other two areas of praise and protection are in place. If you are not protecting and praising your wife, pampering will be seen as bribery in order to fulfill some ulterior motive (I got you flowers, now we can sleep together!). If you have tried to pamper your wife and it has not been received well, take a serious look at your lack of protection.

Pampering involves two aspects: who your wife is, and what she likes. Who your wife is determines what she likes. Because my wife is an active person, she likes gifts that promote activities. Men must tailor their pampering according to who their wife is. If men do not go out of their way to understand their wives and therefore pamper accordingly, it is the relational equivalent to expecting a four-cylinder Corsica to pull a loaded trailer, or hoping a semi can park in the economy row. We will be diving deeper into the aspect of understanding your make and model in the next chapter.

Man Challenge:

Fill out the sheet and specifically praise her for what she has done.

My wife does for me:

1. _____
2. _____
3. _____
4. _____
5. _____

Write out a creative way you could thank her for her sacrifice:

_____

_____

_____

(Examples)

1. She takes care of my kids. Way I can thank or help: Hire a girl from church to babysit once a week.

2. She goes shopping. Way to thank or help: Go with her.

3. She picks garden produce. Way to thank or help: Pull weeds in her flower garden.

4. She does the dishes. Way to thank or help: Buy paper plates.

5. She does laundry. Way to thank or help: Give her a foot rub.

Date Accomplished: _____

Chapter 4
Your Make and Model
Knowing and understanding your vehicle

"What's your make and model?" This is the standard question of all car parts stores when I go in looking for a part to fix my vehicle. It is a logical question and one that should be applied to a marriage relationship. If you do not understand your vehicle, you cannot fix or properly operate your vehicle.

It is your job to know what make you have, and what are some of the individual requirements. This chapter is not going to give you the universal standard on all the possible personalities, but rather give you the tools so you can figure out what are the characteristics of your particular model.

Not all vehicles are alike. If you were to try to interchange the parts from an Audi and put them on a Chevy, you would have serious problems. Every car has quirks and differences, many of which have been pointed out by your mother. One thing that must be understood is that, no matter how hard you try, you will not turn your Ford Fusion into a Peterbuilt. There are many different makes with different options; you chose your particular make and model, and each model is precious and unique in its own right.

Every personality has specific requirements and abilities. A couple of years ago my brother was looking at buying a vehicle, and he found a great deal on a Jeep 4x4 Grand Cherokee. After

The greatest resource you have to understanding your wife is her.

talking with a mechanic friend who found out that the vehicle was primarily going to be used as a commuting car, he talked my brother into buying a less showy Chevy Lumina, primarily due to the fact that Jeeps are expensive to run and expensive to repair.

If I were to ask you which vehicle was better, it would be hard to say, but for my brother's purposes the Lumina was better than a Jeep. Ironically the same friend bought himself a Jeep and spent thousands of dollars in repairs and was never satisfied with it. You may be tempted to wish you had a different model or a "newer" version, but what must be kept in

A good mechanic gets to know his particular machine.

mind is your model will be more than sufficient and will take care of you, if you take care of her. "Let your conversation be without covetousness; and be content with such things as ye have: for he hath said, I will never leave thee, nor forsake thee." (Heb 13:5)

Even though different models require different amounts of care, every personality has the same basic needs. They all thrive on praise, pampering, and protection. Along with these three, every model would benefit from the mechanic reading I Corinthians 13 periodically and applying the principles of true love.

A good mechanic gets to know his particular machine. I get a kick out of listening to my small-town mechanic tell all about my vehicle and what I need to be aware of on my vehicles, and what I should be prepared to replace in the future.

He knows a surprising amount about my vehicle because he is willing to do two things: ask questions, and really observe. The first time I took the vehicle into him, I was bombarded with questions. "How long has it been since you flushed the transmission? Is this the original head gasket? How long has the anti-freeze been low?" After asking the preliminary questions, he took his time looking over the vehicle and did an awful lot of observing. A good husband will get to know and understand his wife. "Likewise, ye husbands, dwell with *them* according to knowledge." (I Peter 3:7)

Man Challenge:

Take time to understand your particular system. Ask your wife about her...

Needs. What are they?

_____

What are her dreams?

_____

What would she like to save money for?

_____

What has she always wanted to do?

_____

Where has she always wanted to go?

_____

What would she like to do with you regularly?

_____

What would she like to see regarding, friends, family, and your relationship?

_____

_____

Date Accomplished: _____

Chapter 5
Tune Ups
General maintenance and inspection
for optimum performance

In order for a car to function properly it needs regular and consistent tune-ups. Tune-ups vary from oil changes to new spark plugs. They are rarely costly, but they save lots of money in the long run. Overall, the time spent on a tune up will save you trouble later on. Tune-ups are designed to allow smoother operation and a longer-lasting vehicle.

Several years ago, our van began to develop a slight quiver in the front axle. The mechanic told us that the bearings were worn, and if I didn't take care of it, it would ruin the tires and eventually the tie rods. I didn't really feel in the mood to spend $150, so I asked how long he thought it would be before it became a major problem. I postponed the minor adjustments until the entire van shook. It cost me over a thousand dollars to repair the struts, tires, and brakes. I learned a powerful lesson that day about preventative maintenance. It must be regular, is always best, saves time, saves headaches, and saves money.

A good mechanic must pay attention and be on the look-out for potential problems before they arise.

If you, as a husband, take the time to do routine inspections of your marriage, the same results are true. Your marriage will not stall on the side of the road because you forgot to check the engine coolant; you will not have to haul your marriage off to a counselor in order to have the engine overhauled. A mechanic must know what to be on the lookout for when tuning up a marriage.

A mechanic cannot afford to do a sloppy job. My father took his vehicle into a tire shop to get his oil changed and have regular tune-ups. He had just gotten the oil changed at the tire shop before taking it into a dealer for some major repairs. After the job, the dealer showed him a black and gray sheet that looked like the bark of an old tree covered in moss and decay, and said, "This is your air filter. It doesn't look like it has ever been changed." My father looked over the inspection sheet of his previous shop and the air filter was checked off as acceptable every time. If you are going to do an inspection, you have to be thorough or else you are wasting your time and preparing for a major problem down the road.

I cannot expect the car to always tell me what I need to know or what the problem is. Too many husbands assume that since there are no real urgent issues, the marriage must be fine. I have ridden in many vehicles that showed no sign of problems but left me stranded on the side of the road because they were not properly maintained.

A mechanic cannot expect the car to fix itself. A squeaky belt needs attention; a broken compressor will not get better on its own. That is why God made you the mechanic. You have been given the awesome privilege of being your wife's protector and maintaining a wonderful marriage. You would never let your wife drive a vehicle that you knew had brake issues and could potentially leave her careening down a cliff. Why not take a little time to inspect your marriage to see if all points are go?

27 Point Inspection

General Maintenance

1.   Tire Wear / Condition Front – Is there excessive wear in her life?   Yes/No

2.   Tire Wear / Condition Rear – Is she wearing unevenly (devoting too much time in areas)?   Yes/No

3.   Condition of Rear Shock Absorbers – Does she handle bumps and changes well? Yes/No

4.   Condition of Front Brakes – Is there excessive squealing when change occurs? Yes/No

5.   Condition of Rear Brakes – Is she able to stop in time (does she need more time to adjust)? Yes/No

6.   Brake, Hydraulic System– Is there enough understanding to allow change? Yes/No

7.   Emergency Brake Adjustment– Is she able to slow down during emergencies? Yes/No

8.   Condition of Wiper Blades – Does she help clarify situations? Yes/No

9.   Clutch Hydraulic System– Does she change gears smoothly?   Yes/No

10.   Condition of Muffler / Exhaust Pipes – Is there excessive foul or destructive language?   Yes/No

11.   Exterior/Paint – Is there excessive grime and salt (stress) eating at her? Yes/No

Engine operation

12.   RPM/Output– Is system running at full capacity?
Yes/No

13.   Torque – Are loads equivalent to torque and engine
capacity?   Yes/No

14.   Engine and Transmission Oil – Is there enough oil
(humility) to prevent excess friction? Has the oil been
checked/changed recently?   Yes/No

15.   Condition of Air / Fuel Filters – Any blockage due to
some hurt or misunderstanding?   Yes/No

16.   Condition of Drive Belts – Does she have motivation
to get jobs done?   Yes/No

17.   Drive Belts Adjustment– Does she have enough
support to accomplish jobs?   Yes/No

18.   Condition of Radiator / Coolant – Does she overheat
(anger) easily?   Yes/No

19.   Condition of Radiator Hoses – Plugged lines or
cracks? Is coolant (God's Word) flowing properly?   Yes/No

Electrical System

20.   Interior Functions and Controls – Is she responsive?
Yes/No

21.   Dashboard lights – Are there any warning signs?
Yes/No

22.   Condition of Battery/Cables – Condition of
Communication. Does she feel free to share her dreams,
feelings, fears? Any corrosion?   Yes/No

23.   Condition of Spark Plug/Wires – Does she have
enough energy?   Yes/No

24.   Head Light Operation– Is she helping illuminate
your goals and dreams?   Yes/No

25.   Stop, Tail, Turn Signal Lights– Is she communicating
accurately (is she sarcastic, condemning, manipulative, shy,
silent...?)   Yes/No

26.   Heater / AC Operation– Is the ride comfortable for
both parties? Yes/No

27.   Other: _____

Required Technician Signature:

I certify that all mechanical items have been inspected.

Technician _____Date: _____

   Some tasks may require outside help. Do you have a trusted mechanic (friend, pastor, counselor) that could honestly evaluate the condition of your marriage? If so, what is keeping you from asking them for assistance?

Chapter 6
Warning Lights
Determining and deciphering the dashboard

I was driving a car back from a car auction when a warning light went off on the dash board, warning me of an issue with my anti-lock brake system. I was aware of the issue before I purchased the vehicle, so I was not surprised. After a few minutes, the dashboard light changed to a warning bell whose insistency echoed constantly throughout the cab. I attributed the noise to a lack of fluid and drove until I was able to go to NAPA and get some DOT 3 brake fluid. After putting in a half bottle, the alarm stopped. I took my prize, which I had purchased at an incredible bargain, to show my wife, and she began to drive the car. Within minutes, the warning bell was back, and I knew that the car I had just bought had serious problems, as the break lines had rusted out completely. This chapter is designed to help the average man decipher, prevent, and fix the dashboard lights and alarms in so many marriages. "It is better to dwell in the wilderness, than with a contentious and an angry woman." (Proverbs 21:19)

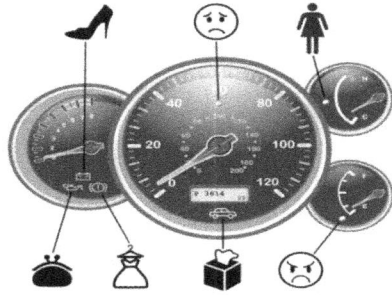

If there are warning lights flashing in your marriage, or loud, incessant noises present, chances are you have not been doing a good job at keeping your marriage maintained. We cannot go back and change that until we fix the urgent problem at hand. Most vehicles come with a manual to help us decipher what the little symbols mean and how to fix them. Sadly, our wives often assume we know what the lights and dinging noises mean.

The signals and symptoms that women use are often confusing because they often come in a different language. What the woman is saying makes perfect sense to her, but men often don't get it. It would be impossible to list all the signals and what they mean, because women often use them interchangeably. Many of the symbols are similar to your vehicle's check engine light. It could mean anything from a corroded sensor to a thrown piston. What we are going to do is learn how to use a code reader and often times be able to get the machine to tell us what is wrong in man language.

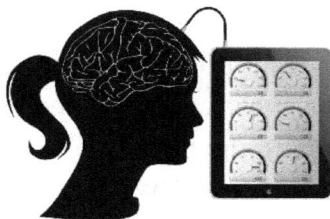

This is not the same as flat out asking your wife what's wrong. If you ask any woman what is wrong, you probably will not get a cohesive (or even honest) answer. Primarily this is due one of two reasons. The woman assumes you already know (and don't care), or the car cannot tell the mechanic what is wrong. In both cases, it is our job as the leader of the home to look into the matter and turn off the warning light.

> **God's greatest tool for changing you is your marriage. Don't fight Him.**

What must be kept in mind is that every problem in a marriage is the husband's responsibility, either because he made the problem or he was not willing to deal with it properly. You may say, "That's not fair, you don't know my wife. She is contentious, nagging, and a bitter backbiter, and those are her good points." Let me ask you, "Have you forced her to nag by not being a good listener? Is she bitter because you have not treated her like God requires? Is she standoffish because you have continually wounded her with a sarcastic, uncaring attitude? Is she unresponsive in bed because you are inconsiderate of her needs at home or in the workplace?" Those types of selfish responses on behalf of your wife are not right; however, they are understandable when a husband fails to realize the pain he is causing.

The typical man model is, "She'll get over it," or "She'll just have to learn I don't work that way..." The Biblical model is Proverbs 28:13, "He that covereth his sins shall not prosper: but whoso confesseth and forsaketh them shall have mercy."

Whether men want to own up to it or not, the fact is, if there is an issue in the home, God is not going to knock on the door and ask to talk to the son or daughter to find out who caused the stress. He is not going to ask the wife why your home and marriage is in shambles. God is going to ask for the person He put in charge, and the buck stops with you. So if there is tension and fighting in your home, it is your God-given role to do something.

I do realize that many issues in a marriage are not because the man made the problem. A woman's past has made her what she is today. There may well be many issues that your wife has that you did not create; however, it is now your God-given role as the head to care for the rest of the body, and help cleanse your wife. This is through gentle application of the water of God's Word to yourself first, and then your wife (Eph 5:23-26).

As husbands we are to wash ourselves first, before we are able to wash our wives. "Husbands, love your wives, even as

Christ also loved the church, and gave himself for it; that he might sanctify and cleanse it with the washing of water by the word." (Eph 5:25-26) A surgeon is not qualified to do surgery on someone else unless his hands are clean. If his hands are dirty, the infection that is spread is often worse than the original disease. "Thou hypocrite, first cast out the beam out of thine own eye; and then shalt thou see clearly to cast out the mote out of thy brother's eye." (Mt 7:5) Once you stand before God having been power-washed, then you are in a position to truly help your wife.

Too many times in life, we as guys get frustrated when we see the warning light and blame the car, or we focus on simply getting rid of the light. We get upset that the wife is always late when it's time to leave, so we blare on the horn and ridicule her until she learns to be a "submissive" wife. I had a car in college that continually showed the fix engine light. I was not willing to spend money to fix it, so I got rid of the warning by putting a piece of black tape over it. My warning was gone, but my problem was not solved, and that vehicle today is currently in the backyard of a mechanic with a blown engine on the bottom of a to-be-fixed list.

You help her remove sin by reflecting the Savior.

If a warning light or noise goes off, don't get upset. Instead of getting angry at the disturbance the light causes, we should be grateful for the warning that allows us a chance to change something before the low oil burns up our engine. The warning light is a woman's way of letting her mechanic know something is wrong.

The lights must not be ignored. If not taken care of properly, they will cause major problems later on. If not addressed, they will affect your operation and performance and leave the operator without a reliable vehicle.

Man Challenge:
Warning Signals and how to decode them.

Remove all distractions for your wife (including kids) and romance her: Take her to a dress-up restaurant, walk to a special place for a picnic, go for a moonlit drive, reserve a night at a bed-and-breakfast, rent a canoe, take a walk through the winter woods with a thermos of coffee or hot cocoa, take her to a coffee shop, go for a bike ride, look at old pictures together, go to a green house, take her somewhere where she will feel special and has no responsibilities.

In your own words, express your appreciation for her beauty as a woman and admit your own failure to understand her properly. Ask your wife if she would help you learn to communicate and understand her better. (Do not tell her she is broken and doesn't know how to communicate. You are the one needing help understanding and asking for her help.)

Without defending yourself, ask her the following questions. In fact, after you ask her a question, staple your lips together.

What do you feel when I am not listening to your needs?

_____

_____

What does it mean when you are very quiet?

_____

_____

When I am ignoring you, how do you try to get my attention?

_____

_____

How can I know if I am the problem or something else is bothering you?

_____

_____

Do not expect this one conversation to fix every problem. This is a simple diagnostic test, so you as the mechanic can decode what the lights on the dashboard mean.

If you want to ruin the entire evening and sleep on the couch, explain away every example and belittle her communication signals and tell her she is confusing. (Yes, women are confusing, but only because men have not taken the time and energy to properly learn their language.)

Date Accomplished: _____

Chapter 7
When You Hear a Funny Noise
Listening to what the vehicle is saying (or not saying)

Wives talk an awful lot. They do not talk for the same reasons guys talk. Guys talk in order to exchange information and get something done. Women talk to express their feelings, share concerns, vindicate themselves, and any other reason they feel like. Talking for a woman is what sex is to a guy. It is the intimate sharing of her being. The same rejection you feel when your wife does not share her body, is the same thing that a woman goes through when her man does not listen. Because women talk, men need to become good listeners.

> **Because women talk, men need to become good listeners.**

Men need to listen for what is being expressed, not simply what is being said. When a woman talks, she is undressing herself emotionally. She is stripping off the hindrances that make her feel bound. A man must know how to listen and help loosen the straps and allow his wife the freedom of speaking unencumbered. Unfortunately, many men cause the wife to cover up by not understanding. The woman, through talking, is trying to uncover herself and wants her man's approval.

Suppose in your next lovemaking episode, your wife told you that you stink, you're obnoxious, and she needs to clean the house! Would that turn you on? That mentality is no different than what so many husbands do to their wives when they are trying to communicate. The wife longs for confirmation and shares her ideas, and the husband immediately shoots his wife down with phrases like, "It would cost too much; you didn't think through it enough; it would be boring..." There are also many non-verbal turn-offs as well: walking out of the room, reading or texting while she is talking, anything short of eye contact... There is no better formula to turn off a woman sexually than to turn her off emotionally.

Men must understand that when a woman shares her most precious soul, it is tender and needs to be protected. When your wife talks, you as the husband must help undress her soul and comment on the beauty you see within.

Previously I have been referring to general conversation. There are times when the husband returns home with nothing on his mind, and then comes the bombshell. Your wife's mascara has formed trenches on her cheekbones as she weeps bitterly. There is probably nothing more that speaks to a man's sense of duty, or his sense of sarcasm, than a woman's tears. Upon finding that both children are still alive, and she has not succumbed to any bodily harm, you realize the tears are a result of a song on the radio. The same principle discussed above must come into effect. Listen! Listen! Listen! Listen to what she is sharing, because she is sharing herself. "He that answereth a matter before he heareth it, it is folly and shame unto him." (Proverbs 18:13)

Just like you have the biological need to get physical, your wife has a need to share her soul. In her time of tears, she is coming to you for the support and care she needs. Repress the urge to fix the situation; nothing may be broken. This aspect is very hard for me, as I am a fixer, a counselor, and daily people are coming to me for advice. If you come up with a solution to "fix" the problem on the fly, your wife will assume one of two things: you do not care enough about her to listen as she undresses her soul, or you think her problem is silly (and, by extension, she is silly).

When a man takes time to listen to his wife, he will not have a hard time knowing how to please her.

Women need vindication of their feelings. They want to know that what they are feeling is normal or at least acceptable. This is why they can spend four hours talking with their girlfriends and never really come to any conclusions. In their tears, they are coming to the only place they know for comfort and support. If you do not give it to them in the form of simply holding and listening intently, it will become a vicious cycle of insecurity as the wife feels she has nowhere to go or begins to look elsewhere for the emotional security she needs. [I should note that emotions and feelings are not a biblical basis for determining truth. Truth comes from God's Word (John 17:17). In context of sharing her feelings, however, your wife has the need to unload her feelings.]

There are times when a solution is warranted or something must be addressed, such as problems with a child at school, but once again Proverbs 18:13 comes into play. A wise husband will listen first and act secondly. It is interesting that as a husband begins to truly listen and seeks to understand his wife, the times of emotional stress and fountains become less and less, because the woman knows she is protected and cared for.

In the event that a solution or decision is truly needed, the time spent listening will add credence to your solution. The wife will be much more willing to submit to someone that has taken the time to deeply listen.

If a wife is sharing, she wants confirmation that you are listening to her. This can come in the form of questions or actions. If she is talking about how stressful her week was and how tired she is, ask her what was the busiest part of her day, if there is anything you can do to help alleviate the stress, etc. Your questions will show that you truly believe that she had a rough day. Your actions might be bringing home a takeout meal for supper. When a man takes time to listen to his wife, he will not have a hard time pleasing her because he knows what matters to her.

> **Women share to connect. So when a woman talks, and a man solves, she hears, "I am broken."**

A husband must listen to and meet the needs of his wife. Just as the rattling or a quiver in a car alerts the mechanic there is an issue that must be dealt with, when a wife talks, a good husband will be listening to the possible cause behind the noise. It is only with this mentality that the seemingly incessant noise becomes discernible and relational.

Man Challenge:

List what you feel are your wife's five greatest needs:

1. _____

2. _____

3. _____

4. _____

5. _____

For a test to see how good you currently have been at listening, go emotionally "undress" your wife, and ask her what she feels her greatest needs are. *If you want to spice up your homework a little, up the stakes and play truth or dare and create intimate consequences for right answers.*

Date Accomplished: _____

Chapter 8
Completing the Circuit
Communicating with the vehicle

Anyone who has worked with electricity understands that in order to produce power, there must be a completion of the circuit. Communication in a marriage works the same way. Not only do men have to be good listeners, they also need to be good communicators. A wife needs to know what you think, particularly in two areas: information and confirmation.

Everything runs more smoothly with proper information. Think of the areas that frustrate you in your marriage: when your wife is continually late, when your wife tears you down in public, spends too much money, nags you about asking for directions or fixing something at home. How many of those areas have you sat down and explained to your wife that they get under your skin? Have you sat down and explained to your wife what you feel? I am not talking about sarcastic jabs about how long it takes her to get her hair and makeup ready but actually sitting down and calmly communicating your expectations with your wife.

Don't expect your wife to know your language.

Don't assume your wife knows how you think or always knows what you want. If you have not taken the time to communicate what you like or that something bothers you, don't expect her to know. Communication takes patience. Just as you are still learning about your wife, she is still learning about you.

The husband who is following God's command in I Peter 3:7 will realize that understanding works both ways. Your wife didn't come with a manual, and neither did you. How is your wife going to understand you and what you like or dislike if you do not tell her? A biblical husband will take the time to explain to his wife how he feels and what he thinks. He will also remember that, just as he often forgets her preferences, so will his wife forget his. Information communication involves sharing the things about you that your wife needs to know.

Secondly, a wife needs confirmation communication. These are the areas your wife needs to know about herself. A woman's disposition is to please, and you as the husband are her confirmer. Just like a child naturally wants the confirmation of his or her father, the wife as a helpmeet desperately desires the approval and confirmation of her husband. Without confirmation, a wife becomes insecure. With time, the unconfirmed wife becomes more unpleasing to her spouse because she is constantly double-checking.

I can't assume my wife knows what I want if I don't tell her.

Women have no way of knowing what goes on in our male, simplistic minds if we don't communicate. If a woman doesn't know if her man is happy or well-pleased with her, she will be insecure and unstable. Imagine if God never told us our standing with Him or that we pleased Him. We would be miserable as Christians.

When was the last time you confirmed your wife and made a specific comment on any of these areas: looks, personality, cooking, mothering, job, love, thoughtfulness, frugalness, compassion, wisdom, tenderness, organization, thoroughness.… Without confirmation, insecurity rises and desire for change comes to a screeching halt. Your wife will be unable to change if she is unsure. Imagine a race where there is no clearly defined finish line or rulebook. Without confirmation, your wife will not know which direction to run or change. Her mind will continually be plagued by thoughts of doubt and unrest. Confirmation assures your wife that she is pleasing you.

Confirmation must be specific. Phrases like, "That was a good meal," or, "You look nice," are general, do not say much to anybody, and show a Neanderthalic effort and vocabulary. Praise her specifically: "I really liked what you did to that roast; it was so tender," or, "I am amazed that you can make such good food with all of your responsibilities." (There is an appendix for those who may need help in this area.)

Confirmation must be genuine. Nothing is more dangerous in confirmation than bribery. Women can spot an ulterior motive in a compliment. If you are hoping to compliment in order to get something in return, you had better bring a blowtorch and a stick of dynamite, because the vault just closed and you will never get into your lady's soul.

Confirmation must be often. A woman's soul is like a fruit tree in an arid climate. If watered abundantly and profusely, it will produce unbelievable fruit, but if water is held back, it will slowly wither under the scorching sun.

Some of you may have read this chapter and thought, "There is no way I am going to humble myself with all this woman talk." There is nothing unmanly about preserving your marriage and your wife. In fact it is the most manly thing you can do. Christ humbled Himself and came down to our level (Phil 2:1-8).

Chapter 9
Listening to Your Vehicle
Learning why the vehicle is making noises (talking)

When I bring my van in for an inspection, my mechanic will often drop me off at work. As I was getting dropped off in my vehicle, my talkative mechanic suddenly got very quiet and missed the turn for my work. I asked if he was going to drop me off, and he apologized and said, "I was just listening to the hum of your vehicle." I was aware of the hum, but thought it was from the new tires on the road. He said, "No, I think something is out of alignment."

If I went into the garage and told the guys that my tires were making noises, they would realize that I am coming with a deeper problem than noisy tires, or else they might suggest I put in earplugs to cancel out the noise. Any good mechanic would listen to my vehicle and then probably run it through some tests in order to confirm the tires are balanced and the shocks and struts are okay. They would listen to the noise in order to determine what was the root cause. Communication in marriage works the same way.

There are three levels of communication: what was heard, what was said, and what was meant. With my mechanic, what was heard was the hum of the tires, (talking about that would not help the problem), what was said was that there is a problem with the tires (focusing on the problem will not fix the problem), and what was meant by the mechanic was, "We need to look at why the tires make noise."

The same type of conversation took place with my wife. When I came home from work, she met me at the door with tears in her eyes and said, "I am sorry the house isn't cleaned."

What was said was, "The house is messy." What her husband heard was, "I feel overwhelmed about the mess." Operating on what I heard, when my wife went shopping, I did the dishes, cleaned up the bathroom, and waited with rapt attention for the praise my wife would give me when she returned. Unfortunately, I did not understand the third level of communication: what was meant. When my wife got home, she began to cry again, and they were not good tears. They were the confusing tears that every husband fears. My wife was trying to tell me she was sorry for being a bad wife. My cleaning the house was actually a bad thing because it aggravated her sense of supposed bad-wife-ness.

The husband must be on the lookout for all three levels of communication. Lack of understanding of this communication principle creates the exasperated, "Honey, what's this about?" From the man's perspective, everything seems great. The wife asks a simple question and suddenly an hour-and-a-half-long discussion takes place. At the end, the man is left bewildered and alone.

We as men try to counter our misunderstanding by appealing to the second level (what we heard). "But, honey, what you said was… I don't do it all the time…. That's an exaggeration…" And in our attempt at communication, we start the cycle all over again until the only way out is the inevitable "Whatever!" Both parties are left with a sense of anger and frustration and decide it is easier to quit trying to communicate.

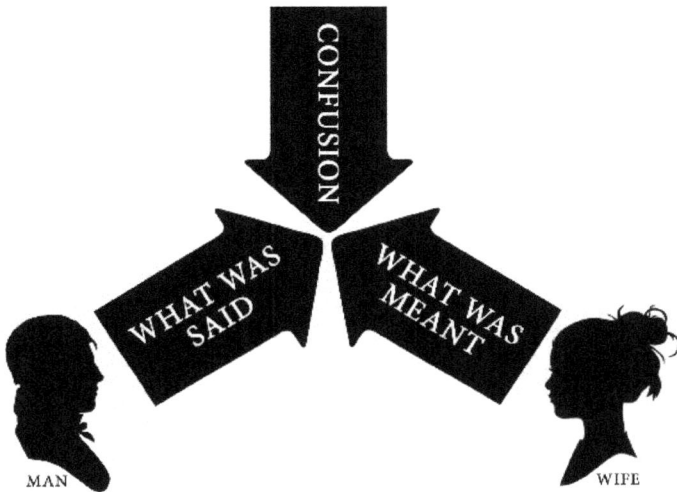

CONFUSION

WHAT WAS SAID

WHAT WAS MEANT

MAN

WIFE

Communication is made more difficult by the fact that women will skip from level to level, often times not being aware of the fact that they are doing so. Women assume men know how to communicate and choose not to.

The facts are, men don't communicate because we do not know how, and when we do, we often times mess it up. After continued failure, the safest route is for us to clam up. If you are feeling lost in this world of communication, there are two nearly magical phrases that will allow you to communicate quickly and genuinely.

The first simple phrase will highlight and alert the man to which communication level is being used. Husbands must learn to ask, "What do you mean by...?" For example: If she says, "I really miss the time we used to spend together," instead of pointing out

Women assume men know how to communicate and choose not to.

that you took off work to remodel her bathroom and she didn't bother to visit with you, ask her, "What do you mean…?"

A secondary phrase that is closely related to the first is, "What I am hearing is…" This involves restating what you thought was said. The beauty of this question is, the wife will begin to understand how guys think, as well as learn to word sentences without underlying assumptions. So often communication crashes because of underlying assumptions that are never addressed. Communication is a two way street.

If used regularly, "What do you mean by…?" "What I am hearing is…?" Will eliminate most miscommunication.

If used regularly and properly, these two phrases (What do you mean?, What I am hearing is…) will eliminate nagging, miscommunication, and heated discussions, and will allow for more productive adventures.

Since so much of communication is nonverbal, the levels of communication must be addressed verbally. This can be difficult because guys are experts at talking with their hands. Actions speak louder than words but are much more prone to misunderstanding. The simple act of walking across the carpet in your boots, because you were in a hurry to take the kid to soccer practice, can and probably will be perceived by the wife at communication level three (what was meant).

To begin to learn how your wife perceives nonverbal communication (action), ask her what she understands you to be saying when you do a manly action that pleases her. After a few ego strokes, blow your wife away with this one question.

"Is there anything I do that bothers you?" This is not the time to defend yourself. This is the time to listen and ask questions for both of you to learn. If you are sure there will be quite a list, ask her, "If there was one thing you would want me to change, what would it be?" Men, if you have not shown a pattern of truly understanding, your wife may not know how to handle this question and may be scared to be overtly honest. Be patient, as you both are learning new communication skills.

There is no one more qualified to tell you how to make her feel like a queen than your wife.

Man challenge

Sit down and explain to your wife that you are trying to become a more understanding husband and need her help. Ask her, "How can I communicate better?" Then take a stapler and clamp your mouth shut and listen. You will ruin everything if you try to defend yourself and explain away her examples.

I can communicate better by:

_____

_____

When she is through, do not give a detailed explanation of what you were thinking, simply admit to her that you now realize you have been hurtful and want her help in changing your destructive habits.

Realize as well that phrases such as "I'm sorry you feel that way," or, "I am sorry you were hurt," do not qualify as apologies. They are actually accusations. "I am sorry, I see now how hurtful **I HAVE BEEN**. I am sorry for being so **SELF-FOCUSED**; I did not realize. Thank you for helping me see **I WAS WRONG**."A simple apology and admittance of being wrong in men seems like a weakness, but it takes more strength to admit failure then to deny it. If we want God's blessing in marriage, we must be willing to humble ourselves before God and our wives. "Humble yourselves in the sight of the Lord, and he shall lift you up." (James 4:10)

Lack of understanding or miscommunication may not be intentional, but according to I Peter 3:7, it is the man's job to fix. Many men pride themselves in never being wrong, but Biblically if you have never apologized to your wife, you are wrong (Proverbs 21:4, 28:13).

Date Accomplished: _____

Chapter 10
Navigational System
How to get where you want to go in a conversation

Google has simplified mankind's life in many ways. Among the world's top 10 inventions is Google Maps (toilet paper holds exclusive rights to #1). I can get directions to pretty much anywhere in the world by typing in my destination, and one more important piece of information: my starting point. Your starting point will determine your ending point. If I were to travel 1,500 miles west, I would end up near Seattle, but if I were already in Seattle and followed the same directions, I would end up somewhere in the Pacific Ocean.

A good husband will understand that women have different starting points. I want you to remember the last time your wife gave you driving directions or told you

> **Your starting point determines your conclusion.**

to just stop and ask for help. How did you feel? Did you feel she was nagging, bossy, or unwilling to trust you? The reason for this tension in communication is the different starting points.

In the above example, your wife more than likely assumed you realized you were lost and therefore needed directions, whereas you may have been trying to conquer a challenge and figure it out on your own. Based on your wife's starting point, she didn't mean any disrespect by offering advice, yet based on your starting point, your wife's suggestion was seen as a lack of trust in your ability. The situation likely spiraled downhill as your wife began to assume you were stubborn, while you assumed she thought you were stupid and incapable. In turn, your wife likely felt you did not value her, or her advice... and nobody was happy.

Failure to understand this principle (your starting point determines your conclusion) is the precursor to a vast majority of marital strife and fights. In the kitchen, the husband walks by and adds a little pinch of seasoning to the pot, and the wife blows her top and complains about being watched over like a hawk. At play, the husband decides on his day off to go out with the guys or work in the garage, upon entering the house the husband finds a cold meal on the table and an even colder wife. In the bedroom, the husband mentions he'd like to have some fun, and the wife has a headache or is too tired, and the man assumes she doesn't love him.

With time, the assumptions grow deeper and more ingrained, and the problem becomes harder to identify. For example, a man often assumes that after a hard day at work, when he gets home he needs to unwind and read the paper, or watch TV. The wife assumes that when the man is home, it is time to hand over the discipline and fix the problems of the day. When both parties are operating on these assumptions, conclusions are made that are inaccurate. The wife assumes that the husband is lazy and does not care about what is happening with the family. The man assumes that the wife is continually nagging and tunes her out.

The problem of assumptions is that they go deeper into a relationship, and their influence spans much broader bounds then the incident taking place. Imagine our TV-watching man realizes that his wife is unhappy with him and determines to make it up to her. After seeing a deal advertised on TV, he gets a baby sitter, reserves a hotel, and takes his wife out to dinner and a show. Throughout the evening the wife seems distant and, with enough prodding, finally admits that she doesn't feel loved, to which the husband replies, "I have no idea what you mean; I gave up a lot to come here tonight. Do you know how much that motel cost? You are impossible to please."

Many husbands have been left out on the couch after bending over backwards, because they did not understand that an assumption had crawled into their romantic evening and went unaddressed. Imagine how you would feel if you and your boss had a fight about how things should operate in your department, and the next week you received the employee-of-the-month award. That is what goes through a woman's mind when her husband doesn't do what she feels should be done, and then he tries to win and romance her. The wife sees it as bribery.

The root assumptions must be addressed. I enjoy martial arts and am trained particularly in Taekwondo. When I first started sparring with the upper levels, they told me I needed to think several moves ahead. By that they meant that I would never have victory if I only blocked to defend myself. I needed to know where the blow was coming from, so I could block and then find the openings in my opponent's guard. Most marriage fights look like my beginning fighting style; they wait for the spouse's blow to come, and then block or wait for a blow of their own. (As a side-note, I am in no way a proponent of beating your spouse; this analogy is purely for illustrative purposes and the author will not be held responsible for the misapplication of this illustration.)

Defense by itself is a terrible way to do anything. If a husband waits for the blows to come, he will constantly be on guard. He will soon feel like his entire relationship, he is waiting for his wife to verbally assault, and that the only option left is to defend himself.

In order to avoid being a punching bag, the understanding husband will seek to learn his wife's assumptions. This is done in two ways: studying your spouse and asking questions. Watch your wife; observe what upsets her (not just things you do). Know when it is her time of the month, observe how she handles stress,

Our actions make perfect sense to us.

and note how her friends or family have been treating her. Wives will act a certain way for a reason. Study your wife and try to figure out what is causing her mood swings, tiredness, coldness, joy, pleasure, etc.

While you are studying her, be asking questions about her expectations. (See man challenge.) The husband is by no means required to meet all of his wife's expectations (there are expectations not based on biblical truth), but he at least should be aware of them. Knowing what your wife expects will be the oil that allows for a smooth transition in any area of your marriage. Not only will learning your wife's assumptions increase romance in every aspect of marriage, it will also be a good starting point for communicating your expectations to your wife.

Man Challenge:

Look back at your last fight and see if you can list the assumptions made, and see if you were busy defending the blows but lost sight of your wife and the issue.

What started the fight? _____

What aspect did I address? _____

Was I only defending myself?   Yes, No

Was I attacking my wife or the issue?_____

What could I have addressed or said that would have helped the situation?

_____

_____

_____

_____

_____

_____

_____

_____

_____

Expectation chart: (My Wife Expects)

When home from work:

_____

When things are broken:

_____

When on a day off:

_____

When with each other:

_____

When disciplining:

_____

When on vacations:

_____

When she goes out with friends:

_____

When she is shopping:

_____

When making love:

_____

Other:

_____

Other:

_____

I have repeated the questionnaire so you can ask your wife the same questions and see if they agree.

As a side note, if you have not been an understanding or good listener, flat out asking your wife what she expects may be a shock to her, and she may at first be afraid to share. Remember, when we open up our dreams and expectations, we are also making ourselves more vulnerable, and women will see that as a sign of trust and, with time, respect our efforts.

Expectation chart: (My Wife Expects)

When home from work:

_____

When things are broken:

_____

When on a day off:

_____

When with each other:

_____

When disciplining:

_____

When on vacations:

_____

When she goes out with friends:

_____

When she is shopping:

_____

When making love:

_____

Other:

_____

Other:

_____

Date Accomplished: _____

Chapter 11
Driving Your Machine
Considerations on operating and driving in bed

If you have been taking care of your vehicle, it will perform when you want it to. A well maintained vehicle is a joy to ride, and the same is true of your spouse. If a woman is properly cared for and cherished, the man is in for a wild ride.

There is nothing a man does better than get physical. Loud trucks, football pads, and guns are about as manly as you can get, and they all involve the adrenaline-pumping action of getting physical. When it comes to sex, men don't need much prep. One look and we are primed and ready for action. Men don't need any explanation or rationale for having sex. It is what we do, and we do it well.

The problem arises when men fail to realize women don't work the same way. This is not bad; it is simply the fact. Dale Earnhardt may have been able to drive a mean racecar, but he would have to have driven a Peterbuilt with a little more caution. Any good trucker knows that, in the winter, you have to let your truck idle for a while before you can take off, and you are not going to go from zero to sixty in 3.5 seconds. If you drove a semi the way you drove a sports car, serious damage would occur.

If you want to have great sex, you need to realize some basic fundamentals about the way a woman works. Women have sex with their entire being. Men have sex with their bodies; women have sex with their heart. Therefore in order for sex to be mutually-fulfilling, the husband must be willing to touch his wife's heart before he touches her body. This is the reason so many husbands have been left bewildered and alone when they try to comfort their spouse with a hand on the shoulder, and their wife tightens up.

Why did God give sex? It is the mutual enjoyment of two people who have given themselves totally to each other. "Let her be as the loving hind and pleasant roe; let her breasts satisfy thee at all times; and be thou ravished always with her love." (Proverbs 5:19)

When done God's way, it should be impossible to tell who is giving and who is taking. This total commitment happens first outside of the bedroom. If I am not willing to give my entire being to my wife, I have no right sleeping with her. If I am asking my wife to give her all to me, and I am not willing to take out the trash, change a diaper, listen deeply, or truly serve her needs, I am robbing from my wife. I am asking my wife for a total and complete commitment, while refusing the same to my wife. I am commanded to give my all to my wife regardless of how she treats me (Eph 5:25).

Sex is the thermometer not the thermostat.

The only thing that stands between a man and making love to his wife is clothes, but that is not how your wife works. A woman cannot let herself go, unless she feels completely safe and cared for. If I am not meeting my wife's needs (emotionally, spiritually, physically), she is not going to want to expose herself to me as her husband, because I have not cared for what she has already given me. If I am unwilling to address an issue that concerns my wife, she will not willingly undress for me. Lovemaking may still happen, but not in a way that is mutually fulfilling.

It must be understood that sex is the thermometer that tells us everything is right in our relationship, but it does not control the temperature. If sex has gotten cold and mundane, it is because the relationship has grown apart. Changing positions or partners is not going to produce any more thrills than moving from the driver's seat to the passenger's will smooth out a bumpy ride on the freeway.

Priming the pump and getting the vehicle ready to "perform" involves continued maintenance, as well as pre-session preparations. Sex begins in the kitchen. Although it is fun to try in the kitchen, that is not what I mean. By the time your wife has washed up smelly children, played cops and robbers, assisted homework, cleaned the dishes, laundry, and put the house in order, she probably is too tired to run another race with you in bed. Asking your wife for intimacy after all that, is the male equivalent to the wife meeting her man at the door when he comes home from work with a honey-do list; you are either too tired or distracted to care which kid hit who, or what broke while you were at work.

If you want good sex, you must make it happen by relieving your wife of her duties. It is very difficult for her to be a maid and a mistress. Kick the maid out of the house, not by telling your wife not to worry about the messy house, but by doing the job of a maid, so your mistress has time to prepare.

Man Challenge:

What tasks around the house could I donate 30 minutes to?

_____ _____

Put your wife in charge of your next love-making session. Tell her you'd like to make love and she is in charge, and you will do exactly what she asks. Give her time to prepare and imagine by leaving her a note, texting her, whispering in her ear before leaving for work, etc.

Ask good questions: If I were to turn you on, how would I do it? How do you want me to touch you? Ask her to make out with you, and tell her you will mirror whatever she does.

Ask her what she would consider an incredibly romantic evening regarding:

Place: _____

Activity: _____

Time: _____

Date Accomplished: _____

Conclusion

After reading this book, some may feel overwhelmed. Let me encourage you. God will never call us to do a task that He has not prepared us for. You may not feel prepared, and that is OK, because God promises to give wisdom to those who humbly seek Him. "If any of you lack wisdom, let him ask of God, that giveth to all men liberally, and upbraideth not; and it shall be given him." (James 1:5)

Others may have read this book out of coercion or to satiate a nagging spouse and may mock the ideas. That's OK too, as I know my words are not inspired. But let me warn you, if the reason for mockery is simply to get out of your God-given responsibility to either repair or care for your wife, you will stand accountable to God, and He will not be mocked. God tells us in Galatians 6:7, "Be not deceived; God is not mocked: for whatsoever a man soweth, that shall he also reap."

Galatians 6:7 is a promise and a warning. If I am willing to unselfishly plant seeds of love, compassion, and understanding, I am bound for an excellent and fruitful harvest in my marriage. However, if I sow to myself seeds of selfishness, irritability and stubbornness, I can be sure my marriage will produce the hard, scabby fruit from the seeds I have sown in a dry climate.

"Likewise, ye husbands, dwell with them according to knowledge, giving honor unto the wife..."

The Beginning...

Appendixes

(Reference to Chapter 3)
Emotions: Plugging a Leaky Gas Tank

If you were to buy a car, and the dealer told you the only problem with the vehicle is that there is a hole on the bottom side of the gas tank, would you buy it? Suppose you did buy it. What would you do about the leak? What if the leak was small, would you still worry about fixing it? Many times there are areas in our marriages that are similar; there are no huge problems, but little drains equal big costs.

"For no man ever yet hated his own flesh; but nourisheth and cherisheth it, even as the Lord the church." (Eph 5:29) I would die before I would let anyone touch my wife, and I am sure the same is true of any self-respecting man, yet daily we abuse our wives and drain the emotional tank with uncaring, thoughtless actions. We beat them up by our self-focused reactions and think nothing of it. If your wife is not protected, you get neglected, yet very rarely will your wife flat out come out and tell you; she will hint and hope you get her suggestions. This is similar to how us guys will "hint" at intimacy and be surprised that our wife doesn't pick up the hints.

If your wife is not protected, you get neglected.

Whether you agree that your wife is cared for financially, emotionally, or otherwise is really not the issue. If your wife feels unprotected, you will be neglected. These signs of an under-protected wife will come in many forms. A wise husband will be on the lookout for an under-protected wife and learn to plug the leak.

The signs of an under-protected wife can include many of the following: lack of sex drive, consistently moping around in her pajamas, indecisiveness, lack of discipline, complaining, excessive crabbiness, unthankfulness, depression, manipulation, neglect, hiding issues, addiction to social media, shopaholicism....

I am not trying to cause you to be reactionary. Some of these symptoms can truly be related to a physical problem, grief, an extenuating circumstance, or appear intermittently (every 28 days). If many of these symptoms become a continual pattern, the neglect you feel is often because your wife has to spend her nurturing energy to protect some area you neglected. This is especially true regarding nagging. Be on the lookout for anything that could be an unnecessary drain spiritually, emotionally, and physically.

If you have a warrior wife, could it be that she just picked up the sword you refused to wield?

There is a scene that is common in too many marriages and that is the issue of turning off the light switch. To some it may not be an issue, but nearly every time I come home, one of my first duties is to go into the basement where nobody has been for the last eight hours and turn off the lights.

Whatever the biological/genetic reason for this phenomenon, the fact remains that women seem to enjoy the useless expenditure of energy and heat. As the sole provider for my family, I am keenly aware of the fact that leaving the lights on, the window open, the hot water running, or the heater on, etc., all cost me money. Now if I were to look at any one of those items, it would not break the bank, yet in my male mind a computation naturally takes place. Three 100 watt light bulbs x 8 hours x $.15 a kWh x 31 days = $11.16 a month, or $131 a year. After I consider the huge expenses in life that are musts (food, shelter, clothing, transportation, etc.), our family can save quite a bit of money by looking out for small expenses and making little changes.

In the same way, we as men are generally pretty good about taking care of the big needs or "bills" of our spouses (protection, financial security, faithfulness), but we stink at taking care of the "little" bills that are draining our wives spiritually, emotionally, and physically.

There are all kinds of little physical drains that life throws at our wives. With a little work, the husband can alleviate huge amounts of strain. Putting your shoes away, hanging up your clothes, leaving a dish rag next to the sink in order to clean up after shaving, picking up groceries on your way home from work, shooting her cat, changing a diaper, make a meal a week, put in a load of laundry, whenever you leave a room pick something up, load the dishwasher, take off your muddy boots before going on the carpet, tucking the kids in at night, folding laundry while watching a movie, giving massages.

These jobs are just as manly as dropping a transmission or overhauling your wife's car and will be met with stunned awe by your lady. This is by no means an exhaustive list; each woman will have her own "list" and is the greatest source of information. I have simply listed a few general starters.

Emotional needs are a little bit harder to meet, as guys are generally more wired for action. Take heart. One benefit of helping a woman physically is that they will translate a lot of that into emotional strength (the exchange process is sort of like spending American money in Canada). Emotional suggestions include: stopping what you are doing to look at your wife when she is talking, sweet words of adoration and confirmation, expensive impractical gifts like flowers, random phone calls, texts, cards at work, lingering kisses before bed (be careful, may lead to not sleeping), random dates.

Spiritually, God designed the man to be the head of the home (Eph 5:23). It is an immense responsibility and requires strong, sturdy shoulders. Sadly, many women are the spiritual heads of the house, whether by choice or default. It is a sad commentary on any marriage when the wife has to lead the family spiritually. There are many ways to help cultivate the spiritual atmosphere in your home: Take the lead in bringing your family to church, ask questions in the car or dinner table, lead in family devotions, study the Scriptures yourself, talk to other godly men, purchase godly CD's or download messages, purchase God-centered books, pay for ladies' or men's conferences, or go on marriage retreats.

Many women are the spiritual heads of the home by default.

We as men should emulate Paul's exhortation in Philippians 2:1-8. In order to be great leaders we need to be great servants. Christ not only meets our huge need of salvation from sin, but He also takes care of our lesser needs and wants (Lu 12:7).

(Reference to Chapter 8)
Communication: Praise Pays

Engines can perform above their rated capacity with a slight alteration in their fuel. If you want a wife that you can hardly keep up with and is capable of amazing things, praise will leave the afterburners burning long into the night.

Praise wins out over critique. It is inevitable that two people living together in a house are going to want to see change in the other person. Instead of a sarcastic comment about the dirtiness of the kitchen or not having enough clean socks, try positive statements that praise your wife for what she has done well. Here are a few suggestions: Leave notes on the bathroom mirror with erasable marker; put thank you notes on the laundry basket, sink, stove, lingerie drawer; tell the kids what an amazing mom they have; leave signs of appreciation in her workplace (sticky notes or dollar bills in the drawers). A woman who hears affirmation and praise will remember what means a lot to her man.

Praise who she is. Men like to be praised for brute strength and manly things; ladies like to be praised for womanliness. Observe what means a lot to your wife and praise her for it. Actions or phrases like, "This is my woman," holding hands, putting your arm around her waist, giving her a peck on the cheek, reaching over and giving her a squeeze, getting the car door for her, telling others how she completes you, bragging about things she has done recently, (never tell embarrassing jokes or stories without her permission), warming up the vehicle, completing a honey-do-project, or making a personalized bumper sticker with a message for or about her.

These are suggestions; make sure the praise comes from you and that the praise will be well-received from her point of view. Do not draw attention to what she is sensitive about. If she is sensitive about her weight or cooking ability, don't draw attention to it. Drawing attention to failure, particularly in looks, would be the equivalent to failing a driver's exam for a guy.

Do not forget that, to every negative trait, there is a positive aspect. Your wife may be super emotional, but the flip side is she is very caring with your kids; she may be very talkative and opinionated, showing she has strong character and beliefs. Write out a list of the traits that may annoy you about your wife, and in the other column write out the plus of those traits. Like it or not, your personality traits also have negatives. "Let your moderation be known unto all men. The Lord is at hand." (Php 4:5)

Be specific in praise. "You look nice tonight," is a sloppy way of expressing your feelings. A wife will often spend hours planning and preparing herself or a meal. She wants to know specifically what you like. Women will feel particularly slighted if you hardly notice or express what she did to her hair, and then you pass a muscle car on your way out to eat and you know all the specs including model, year, and engine size.

There is another sort of praise that should be listed, and this is indirect praise. Indirect praise allows your wife to know she is being thought about without telling her. Consider placing a picture of her on your dashboard, computer, cell phone lock screen, or other place of prominence. How would you feel if your wife kept a picture of her ex-boyfriend? This is no different for a woman than when she is less prominent than your dream truck, mount, or boat. Women are very in tune with this secondary praise.

Another way to praise is the giving of time. What you put your time into is what you feel matters. So when you work long hours away from home, you may feel you are being responsible and taking care of your family, whereas she feels neglected. If you had an employee that continually showed up late for work, you would conclude he does not care about work, and probably fire him. The same is true in marriage. If you continually "show up late" for home or don't give your wife an idea of when you will be back, the wife sees it as you not being willing to show up for marriage. This is the same idea Jesus expressed in Matthew 6:21, "For where your treasure is (time, talents, etc.), there will your heart be also."

Your wife views your time as an extension of yourself.

Just like you don't really buy the continual excuses your employee might give about a rough weekend or car problems, your wife is not going to buy your excuses about your absence of time. You may feel that putting in an extra 30 hours of work is honorable, and everyone knows you as a dedicated worker, but your wife will see you taking her time and giving it away.

I was made aware of this principle when I was going to work out. My wife has often praised me for my dedication to the gym and physical fitness. So one night after I tucked my wife in with a foot rub, I told her I was going to work out. She opened her half-asleep eyes and slowly said, "Ok." I thought she would be pleased because I had already given up the previous night's workout to watch a movie with her. After I stood up, I looked at my beautiful lady and then crawled into bed. She said, "I thought you were going to work out?" I didn't have to say anything; my very presence told her she was more important, and let's just say I was greatly rewarded for putting my wife first.

Man Challenge:

Am I willing to commit to truthful and meaningful praise on a daily basis?   Yes/No

I will specifically praise my wife regarding her:

Actions, Appearance, Adoration, Activities, Attentiveness

I will look for specific areas my wife shows me God:

_____

I will praise her in public by:

_____

_____

I will praise her in private by:

_____

_____

Date Accomplished: _____

(Reference for Excessive Anger)
Minimizing Friction and Maintaining Oil Pressure

The job of oil is to lubricate. Marriages that get low on oil will burn out quickly and seize up. As in any vehicle, the oil needs to be changed and monitored regularly to help with smooth operation. In order to understand and lead his wife, every man must be aware of several signs of low oil.

The surest sign of low oil is tension. "Only by pride cometh contention."(Proverbs 13:10) If your speech billows out smoke or your stomach ties up in knots after a "discussion," you can be sure there are two proud people, and you are burning oil. If this continues and there is no new oil added (compassion, grace, understanding, forgiveness, forbearance, empathy), you had better upgrade your marriage AAA towing plan because your insistence on being right may leave you stranded.

> **Every man must ask himself,**
> **"Is being right, worth losing my wife?"**

Another sure sign of low oil is defensiveness (Prov 18:2). If your wife is very defensive, she feels insecure. This insecurity will not just stay in the confines of an argument or disagreement. It will affect every area of your marriage, including the bedroom.

Why are people defensive? In short, we defend when we feel threatened. A wise husband must show through actions and words that Jesus is the only true defender in his life (Rom 8:33). Focusing on Christ will allow us the tenderness and compassion our wives truly need and desire.

We as men need to be very aware when our wives are defensive, because it shows a very deep heart issue. Whenever defensiveness appears, the man must first search his own heart to see if there is a self-seeking, sinful heart attitude of attack and defensiveness in his own life (Mat 7:1-6).

> **When we realize that Jesus is our defense, we do not have to intimidate others to feel safe.**

We must also take an honest look at how we handle a critique or correction from our wives. We as guys understand the defensive strategy. We justify our defensive responses to gain respect. *"I had a reason for what I did. If I can only explain to her what I was thinking, she will come around and see that I am not stupid."* When we continually defend ourselves, we are trying to gain the respect of our wives. The problem is, when I defend myself, I take down my wife. (Every point for me is a point against her.) She then feels the need to defend herself, and the circle continues. When a man defends himself to gain respect, he will lose it faster than he can defend (I Peter 2:20-21) and friction continues.

> **You don't fight for something that is not important. In the battle of words, does your wife know she is?**

A wise husband sees this principle and is willing to take one for the team. If you are willing to administer the oil of humility and seek your wife's good over your defense, your engine will run much smoother. This is the idea Paul shares in Philippians 2:3: "Let nothing be done through strife or vainglory; but in lowliness of mind let each esteem the other better than themselves."

Defensiveness needs the added oil of compassion and understanding. Your wife may be struggling through something not involving you, but if you push it, the angst may be taken out on you. As a sidebar, never push an engine when it is low on oil.

A wise mechanic will monitor his system, noting the times in life that burn more oil (family reunions, school days, PMS, social/work pressures, etc.), and be prepared to add some understanding during times of extra stress and pressure. He will not address the issue of a late meal when he is hungry, comment on the messy house after stepping on a Lego, or complain about spending too much money while carrying in groceries.

My wife has illustrated this principle to me. She pays attention to the days in life that are harder for me. As a quick example, the 15th of the month is when the majority of our bills are due. Because she knows this is a high stress day, she spends extra time making my favorite meal.

Another sign of low oil is clamming up. Many men will clam up either because they do not know what to say or are afraid to speak because of their own reaction. If a woman is quiet, the oil is dangerously low. Anger that is repressed will turn into silence, depression, and manipulation.

If your wife has quit bringing issues to your attention, or continually fails to share important details with you, her defensiveness has gone underground. Like the slow leak of a hardened rubber seal, this clamming up will drain your engine.

This clamming up is normally brought about by failure to see the low oil signs. If you have brow-beaten, intimidated, and belittled your wife and her opinions, there is no way she is going to automatically open up, because you have trained her for years to not feel safe in doing so. If lack of maintenance has gotten this far, do not expect instant results. Apologize to your wife for the specific ways you put yourself first, and bring forth actions worthy of repentance. During this time of waiting, trust in God to work in you and your spouse. After all, He is more concerned for the wellbeing of your marriage than you are.

Have your words and actions shown your wife that it is safe to open up?

Monthly Tune-Up:

Instructions: A monthly tune up is a great way to help your vehicle perform at maximum capacity. Each month, the husband and wife fill out the sheet separately, before taking turns verbally sharing each line. Although the questions allow for great discussion, do not take any longer than it would take to heat up a pizza.

Remember, this is a diagnostic tool to help you understand each other. The wife must remember that this is not a dump time, and the husband should remember, this is not a fix time. It may be tempting (especially during the first few tune-ups) to defend. The couple should reserve the right of clarification (what do you mean by...?) but not defense.

The tune-up is a fantastic way, especially for the wife, to be able to express her thoughts in an organized and consistent manner. Those who have completed this form normally find that the wife will have a lot more to share. I would caution the husband not to feel attacked, and remind the wife not to feel slighted that the man doesn't feel the need to share as much. Simply realize your God-given conversation differences, and go eat the pizza.

Start by holding hands and praying.

<u>Spiritual Growth</u> –

    1. Do I feel we are growing together? (Yes/No)

        _____

    2. What main idea am I learning in my devotions?

        _____

    3. Areas of growth I see in my spouse:

        _____

    4. Ideas for family devotions I'd like to implement:

        _____

    5. Areas of spiritual concern:

        _____

        _____

        _____

        _____

Intimacy –

    1. Do I feel my needs are met? (Yes/No)

        _____

    2. Am I being faithful with my eyes? (Yes/No)
    3. Am I being faithful with my mind? (Yes/No)
    4. I love it when…

        _____

        _____

5. I would like to try…

_____

_____

Finances –

1. Are we giving God a minimum 10% of our income? (Yes/No)
2. Do I think we are spending wisely? (Yes/No)

_____

_____

3. I would like to save for...

_____

_____

4. Ways to be more conservative:

_____

_____

5. Ways to minister with our funds:

_____

_____

Parenting –

1. Do I feel we are united in our parenting? (Yes/No)

_____

_____

2. Is there a specific problem with one of our children that needs to be addressed?

_____

_____

3. Is there a specific problem with the in-laws that needs to be addressed?

_____

_____

4. Specific ways we can show our children love:

    _____

    _____

5. What characteristic of God do our kids most see
    in us? _____

6. What characteristic could I work on more?

    _____

7. Ways to improve our parenting:

    _____

    _____

Communication –

1. Have we been doing our
    monthly tune-ups? (Yes/No)
2. Do I speak with gentleness
    and patience? (Yes/No)
3. Do I clam up because I'm afraid to share my
    thoughts, etc.? (Yes/No)
4. Do I feel listened to? (Yes/No)
5. On a scale of 1-10, how often do I feel interrupt-
    ed? (1 2 3 4 5 6 7 8 9 10)

6. Are there ways in which I feel left out? (Yes/No)

    _____

    _____

7. Husband answers the following:

    a. Do I feel disrespected by any actions?

    _____

    b. I feel respected when…_____

    _____

    c. Do I feel free to lead? (Yes/No)

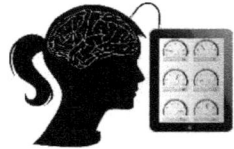

74

8. Wife answers the following:

   a. Do I feel unloved by any actions?

   _____
   _____

   b. List activities that I understand as love.

   _____
   _____

   c. Do I feel I can follow? (Yes/No)

9. Is there anything bothering me I would like to share?

   _____
   _____
   _____
   _____

Health –

1. Are we taking good care of ourselves physically?
   a. Eating right (Yes/No)
   b. Physical exercise (Yes/No)
2. Ways to improve our overall health:

   _____
   _____

3. Concerns I have for my health:

   _____
   _____

Dating –

1. Do you feel we spend enough time together? (Yes/No)
2. New ideas for a date I find interesting include...

   _____
   _____
   _____
   _____

3. Dates we should not do again include...

   _____
   _____

4. Ways to improve quality of time together:

   _____
   _____

5. Two traits I love about my spouse:

   _____
   _____

Things to consider/change before next tune-up (This is for individual reference and does not need to be shared)

   a. _____

     _____

   b. _____

     _____

**Hold hands and each of you pray,
bringing tune-up to a close**

www.ingramcontent.com/pod-product-compliance
Lightning Source LLC
Chambersburg PA
CBHW061503040426
42450CB00008B/1462